Claim the Flame

A Series of Seven Two-Character Dialogues
featuring
The Apostle Paul
and his
1st Century Church Contemporaries

> WARNING:
> This work contains whimsy and historical inaccuracies. Not for academic consumption.

Larry Moeller

Parson's Porch Books

Parson's Porch Books

Claim the Flame: A Series of Seven Two-Character Dialogues featuring The Apostle Paul and his 1st Century Church Contemporaries

ISBN: Softcover 978-1-951472-05-4

Copyright © 2015 by Larry Moeller

All rights reserved. No part of this book may be reproduced or transmitted in any form or by any means, electronic or mechanical, including photocopying, recording, or by any information storage and retrieval system, without permission in writing from the author.

Unless otherwise designated, Scripture quotations are taken from the HOLY BIBLE: NEW INTERNATIONAL VERSION®. © 1973, 1978, 1984 by International Bible Society. All rights reserved.

NRSV. When designated as NRSV, the Scripture quotations contained herein are from the New Revised Standard Version Bible, copyright 1989, by the Division of Christian Education of the National Council of Churches of Christ in the U.S.A. All rights reserved.

To order additional copies of this book, contact:

Parson's Porch Books
1-423-475-7308
www.parsonsporch.com

Parson's Porch Books is an imprint of Parson's Porch & Company (PP&C) in Cleveland, Tennessee. PP&C is an innovative non-profit organization which raises money by publishing books of noted authors, representing all genres. All donations from contributors and profits from publishing are shared with the poor.

Claim the Flame
A Series of Seven Two-Character Dialogues
featuring
The Apostle Paul
and his
1st Century Church Contemporaries

F

"I have had the privilege of knowing Larry Moeller for many years. My first contact was the result of interest he expressed in how a church I led was starting new churches. We met over coffee to chat about church, the mission of Jesus Christ, and how to effectively take the witness of the church into the unreached regions of our back yards. What began as a conversation regarding church philosophy blossomed into a friendship built around the grace-filled message of Jesus.

"In our times together I have always admired his deep relationship with God. I have appreciated his willingness to reflect on and apply the insights God gives him through his meditative approach to scripture. He is one of those unique folks who can bring the truth of God's word into the realm of current society. He knows the words that were written centuries ago must echo into the life canyons of today. What God spoke to the founders of the faith must speak to those of us who have placed our faith in the Savior they declared, defended, and delighted in.

"These sermon dialogues, *Claim the Flame*, are an example of this. Larry takes us into conversations between Paul and his contemporaries to provide glimpses into how they fleshed out their faith stories. The words contained in these personal interactions allow us to step back into history. And it is in our stepping back we discover stuff we can use to step forward in life today.

"Bridges must be built to span the chasm between the history of the faith and our current faith. These seven dialogues help to build those bridges.

"I encourage you to build those bridges. Incorporate these into the life of your congregation. Use them to help your congregants grasp the richness of faith. The result will be clearer understanding, greater faith, and deeper commitment to Christ and his church."

The Rev. Dr. Phil Stevenson
District Superintendent

Pacific-Southwest District of The Wesleyan Church

[Phil Stevenson is the author of The Ripple Church containing practical tips to guide your church into becoming a multiplying church. He also writes a bi-weekly leadership blog, The Rock in the Pond, located at http://thesisugroup.org/blog/.]

Commentary

"Starting and growing a church is a difficult process. It requires a group of dedicated people aligned in mission, but things happen that create road blocks. Often a church tries to find someone who can help. *Claim the Flame* is a fictional series depicting a modern church reaching out to the Apostle Paul, the greatest church builder of all time. They do so by writing a letter to Timothy, who is the next generation Paul grooms to continue the work of growing the church. The letter implores Timothy to ask Paul to be a keynote speaker at the 60th anniversary celebration of the church. Writing from the future means a translation into the time of Paul. We see in this fictional setting how Paul seeks advice and information from a close circle of friends. *Claim the Flame* lets us imagine how a church today can learn by stepping into the lives of Paul and his friends by digging deeply into the Acts of the Apostles and his letters."

Ned E. Clapp, Jr.

[Ned Clapp retired in 2001 after a distinguished engineering career at Oak Ridge National Laboratory. He is a charter member of Farragut Presbyterian Church in Farragut TN, which recently celebrated its 30th anniversary. He served as an elder on the first session, and three more terms over the years. He has co-chaired the New Member Development and the Pastor Care committees. Most remarkably, he has taught the adult Bible Study Sunday School class for all thirty years of the congregation's life.]

Claim the Flame
Introduction

"How can we celebrate the upcoming anniversary milestone of the church and also make it a springboard into the future God intends?"

Therein, the challenge to the planning committee.

And so, 'mission moments' opened Sunday worship on alternating Sundays, beginning the Sunday after Easter. Mission moments included remembrances of past, and highlights of present, ministries.

But how to glimpse the future, and build excitement? Might something be learned by taking a closer look at the experiences of the church's namesake, the apostle Paul? 'Fan into flame …' became the year-long theme, drawn from Paul's encouragement to Timothy, *to fan into flame the gift of God which is in you … for God did not give us a spirit of timidity, but a spirit of power, and of love, and of self-discipline.*
(2 Timothy 1:6-7)

'Nudge' cards were designed and distributed; prayers were uplifted. All were encouraged to fan into flame the Spirit-gift within them through prayer and personal devotion – and to use the cards to share how the Holy Spirit was nudging them to God's intended purpose for their lives. Not the church's purpose, but God's purpose.

And so evolved a Celebration seven-part sermon series: once-a-month two-character skits featuring the apostle Paul in dialogue with his Biblical contemporaries: Timothy, Peter, Lydia, Luke, the Ethiopian eunuch, and Eunice.

The Celebration series presented fun and fascinating encounters with Paul through the lens of artistic license and a bit of whimsy. Scripture texts for the sermon dramas followed Lectionary Year A for the first Sundays of the seven months May through November.

Enthusiasm grew as the culminating Celebration worship and banquet approached on the first Sunday of December. The keynote dignitary brought the sermon message – along with greetings and a personal message from Timothy who, regrettably, was unable to attend the celebration in Paul's stead.

Adaptation and Permission

The scripts which follow are easily adaptable to any church context, and especially well-suited for churches bearing the name of St. Paul.

Claim the Flame scripts in 8-1/2 x 11 format are available through www.risenindeed.com.

Permission to reproduce and adapt for congregational use may be requested through www.risenindeed.com.

- -

Royalties from this book benefit the endowment fund of St. Paul Evangelical Lutheran Church in Maryville, Tennessee – the church for whom the original series was written.

Table of Contents

Dialogue #1	The Invitation (Paul and Timothy)	13
Dialogue #2	A Power Full Pair (Paul and Peter)	23
Dialogue #3	The Color Purple (Paul and Lydia)	35
Dialogue #4	Doctor's Diagnosis (Paul and Luke)	45
Dialogue #5	Doubt (Paul and the Ethiopian eunuch)	55
Dialogue #6	Women of Faith (Paul and Eunice)	65
Dialogue #7	Whom Shall I Send? (Paul and Timothy)	77
Monologue	Greetings and Encouragement (a letter from Timothy)	89

Dialogue 1: *The Invitation*
(Paul and Timothy)

Characters: Paul, the biblical apostle, dressed in the garb of the 1st century church. A bearded, older man.

Timothy, Paul's young protégé, dressed similarly. At least a generation younger.

Setting: In the front of the worship center. The setting is in a private home or conversation nook in a café or coffee shop. A dialogue between two men. The congregation eavesdrops on the conversation.

Props: Two tall stools a comfortable distance apart at stage center, front. The stools are of sufficient height so that the actors, when seated, are clearly visible to all in the audience.

Two music stands to hold each script, at a height unobtrusive to the audience.

Two headpiece or standing microphones, one for each actor.

Texts: 2 Timothy 1:6-7; 1 Corinthians 3:3-11

Adaptation: *Modify all underscored dialogue to adapt to local context.*

[The characters approach center front from opposite sides. There is evident warm collegiality between them as they embrace in greeting … two cherished friends who have been apart for months.]

Timothy:
Greetings, Paul. It is so good to see you again. We've been apart too long. How was the journey? And how are things with our friends in Corinth?

Paul:
Grace and peace to you, Timothy, my friend … from our Lord and Savior, Jesus Christ and from all the believers in Corinth. I bring their warm greetings and especially from Crispus and Gaius, and Stephanus. Every time I am with them, they give thanks for their baptism and how the Holy Spirit changed their lives that day!

Timothy:
Yes, I remember. And when your travels take you back, please give them my love as well.

How is the church there? I hear good things, but sometimes I hear there is arguing. Is everything ok?

Paul:
Oh, everything is normal. Even families argue sometimes, you know. They tell me that even in the strongest of marriages, people argue … though I'm no expert on that. Marriage and family was something I just didn't have time for. And I don't think God has that in my plans, now that I'm getting so old. Yes, I know … miracles can happen. But I don't think God would do such a thing to a woman. Can you imagine any woman who would want to be married to me?

[He chuckles.] *Even I wouldn't want to be married to me!*

Timothy:
[Laughing.] *I sure wouldn't! You're too opinionated and stiff-necked. Maybe it's some of that old Pharisee coming out!*

[Both … more laughter]

How goes the business? The last I heard, you were in Damascus for almost a year, working on a home for Ar-mahn', a son of Shiek Kah-mahl'. Did Ar-mahn' take more wives?

Paul:
Yes ... at last count, I think there are twenty-two. It takes a lot of tents for that big of a clan. Those are nice orders to get, and I'm grateful that people recommend my leatherworking. But it is always a challenge when I get a big order like that, because sometimes it gets in the way of my real work. You know, spreading the news about the Christ to all who haven't heard.

But enough of that.

So, what is the important matter which brings me here? All Crispus would say is that a messenger was asking about me ... and that you needed to see me as soon as possible. Ar-mahn' was firm that I had to finish the last nursery tent before the rains. I came as quick as I could.

What's wrong? You look fine. Is Eunice ok? Or has something happened to Lois?

Timothy:
Oh, no. Mom and Grandma are fine ... nothing like that.

It's just that I received a letter last month from far away, and it has been troubling me. It's written in a strange language, and it took me a while to figure it out. But most important, they talk about you. And they have asked me to speak with you on their behalf. They want you to come and visit them.

Paul:
Visit them?

What do you mean, 'from far away'? And what language? You know that I speak Hebrew and Greek and Aramaic, and Latin from my time in Rome. Those are the only languages that matter. It must be Latin, or you would know it. Let me see it ...

Timothy:
No, *it's not Latin.* [He gives Paul the letter.] *It is a Celtic language, the experts say.*

It comes from a church across the Great Sea of the West ... <u>in a place near the Mountains of Smoke they call Teh-nah'-see</u>. I've asked all around, and all I have learned is that it is very far away. Some of the sea captains in Joppa say they have heard of the land, but they don't know anyone who knows the way.

[Paul is listening ... and studying the letter intently.]

Paul:
[Handing the letter back to Timothy.] *What do they say? What do they want?*

Timothy:
It tells the history of the church near <u>the Mountains of Smoke</u> and how it got started years ago. They are planning a big celebration <u>during the winter solstice</u>, and they want you to come and give the keynote address.

Paul:
Yes, I have heard about the Celtics starting churches in faraway places ... but this is the first I've heard of <u>the Mountains of Smoke</u>. But why do they want me? Why not you – or Silas, or John Mark? Or Peter?

Timothy:
[Chuckling] *Well, the history is very interesting. Let me read a little of it, and you will see why they want you. But I can guarantee that you're not gonna like that part ...*

Paul:
[Exasperated] *What do you mean, I won't like it?*

Timothy:
Just listen, while I read parts of it –

It begins like many of yours ... "Grace, mercy and peace from God the Father and Christ Jesus our Lord."

Paul:
Well, I like that part!

Timothy:
[Glares at Paul ... and then continues reading]

It's very long. I'll touch on the important parts. They talk about dates and times which don't make sense, but it must be their way <u>in the land of Teh-nah'-see near the Mountains of Smoke</u> ...

Let's see ...

<u>*April 23, 1953. An informational supper in a home to explore the start of a church. A pastor from a church in a nearby city presided over the meeting. The names of thirty believers had been gathered at a meeting of the presbyters in the area, and most of them came to the supper in that home. They decided after supper to form an organizing committee*</u> *...*

[Timothy stops reading and looks up] *This is a strange word, 'committee'. The letter is from a 'Celebration Committee'. And all through the letter, they talk about 'committees'. It sounds like they have found a different way to do church <u>near the Mountains of Smoke</u>.*

[He continues reading ...] *Let's see ... yes, '<u>to form an organizing committee comprised of seven people, who elected a chairman and a recording secretary.</u>*

<u>*Two weeks later, on May 10, 1953, they held their first worship at the Village Community Center. A preacher from the nearby city gave the sermon, entitled 'A Church is Born'. There were 33 people there.*</u>

<u>*The next Sunday, May 17, 1953, was very important. They worshiped in what would become their first regular church building. After the service ended, they had a meeting to hear the suggestions of names for the new church from the organizing committee. The names offered were St. Stephen, and St. Mark, and Good Shepherd. After much discussion, one of the youth suggested a different name ... St. Paul. Because they felt that it would be important to tell the story of the church in the community, the name was picked: St. Paul Evangelical Church.*</u>

Paul:
[Loudly] *Ahhhrrgghhhhh!!!! No!!!!*

Timothy:
I told you, you wouldn't like it!

Paul:
No!!!! I keep telling churches all over ... they want to name their church after Apollos, or after Peter, or Barnabas, or you. It is not about us!

Remember, Timothy? Remember how I told the churches ... that I planted the seed, and Apollos watered, but it is God that makes them grow??

And yet, more and more, we hear of churches having names after some of us. I guess we won't be able to stop it ... but it sure rankles me!

Timothy:
[He shakes his head slowly, with a sad look. Then, he continues.]

Let me read more ... it is very interesting.

[He continues reading ...]

<u>The first pastor was temporary and served for 8 months. In January, 1954 there was a special service when the new altar, made by the men of the church, was dedicated. In March 1954, the new church was officially recognized as a mission field and welcomed its first fulltime pastor to serve as Mission Developer.</u>

<u>December 5, 1954 was a very important day. On that day, St. Paul Evangelical Church was formally organized as a congregation. At the organizing worship, 78 members were officially recognized as 'charter members'. At that service, 14 people were baptized ... 7 babies, and 7 adults.</u>

Paul:
Oh, how beautiful when God adopts new children. In baptism, everything changes. I like how it is said in many churches, and even when I baptized you: "Timothy, you have been sealed with the Holy Spirit, and marked with the cross of Christ forever."

Timothy:
Yeah, I'll never forget the words in that second letter you sent me a few years ago. You said: "For this reason I remind you to fan into flame the gift of God, which is in you through the laying on of my hands. For God did not give us a spirit of timidity, but a spirit of power, and of love, and of self-discipline."

Paul:
Yes, dear son ... how important to remember that power that God has put within us. I see far too many people who have that spark inside them, but they let timidity keep it from becoming a flame. Timidity in believing is one of the biggest threats to spreading the Good News of the love of God in Christ Jesus. Remember that, Timothy. Timidity is the biggest threat. Believers must 'claim' the flame ... 'claim' the gift of the Spirit that is within them.

Timothy:
[Thoughtful ... then continuing] *The letter goes on to tell about some of those early years.*

In June 1955, the first regular pastor was called. Growth was slow. In 1957, the church established its first building fund, of $2,500 ... and churches from across the region gave $1,000 toward it. A little after that, a new pastor arrived, and by 1958 there were 89 baptized members. The church went through a few years of pastor turnover and attendance slipped. Finances were tight, so the congregation stopped renting the church building and worshiped in the parsonage for a while. In the spring of 1960, they hit a low ebb when only 8 members communed one Sunday. For several months, they worshiped at a community center, but eventually were told they could no longer worship there.

At that time, a nearby congregation offered the use of their church on Sunday evenings, so Sunday School was at 4:00pm and worship at 5:00pm. In 1961, the first Junior Choir sang for Easter in new robes made by mothers. 'Forward March' was adopted as the theme for the congregation as they began to make plans to build a new church building. Ground breaking was held on Sunday, April 29, 1962 ... and the first worship in the new building was on December 16 that year.

Paul:
Well, it seems the winter solstice is always an important time in the life of that church. I can see why they want to celebrate at that time this year, too.

Timothy:

There's a lot more here, Paul. We can talk more about it tomorrow after you've had some rest. But I'd like to get a letter off soon to them, to let them know when you might arrive. What do you think?

Paul:

I don't know. There is a lot to think about, and I'm not sure I should be the one to go. I want to talk to a few people first, while I'm here.

Timothy:

Who do you want to talk to? Barnabas and John Mark are in Asia, and I haven't seen Luke for quite a while. I guess he's been busy with his doctoring ... and, they say, he's been doing a lot of writing.

Paul:

I don't know. But it's been a couple years since I've talked with Peter. He's traveled a lot, too, and he may know more about <u>this land of the Mountains of Smoke</u>.

I want to make sure that whoever ends up going will be able to speak with authority about how the church is growing ... and how important it is for every believer to 'fan into flame' this gift of the Spirit ... to claim this Spirit of power, and of love, and of self-discipline.

I'll return after I've talked to a few people.

[He embraces Timothy]

Until then, may the Lord be with your spirit.

Timothy:
And also with you.

[They depart.]

Dialogue 2: *A Power Full Pair*
(Commemorating Pentecost)
(Paul and Peter)

Characters: Paul, the biblical apostle, perhaps dressed in a robe resembling the garb of the 1st century church. A bearded, older man.

Peter, the apostle and disciple, dressed similarly. But he is clean shaven.

Setting: In the front of the worship center. The setting is a public café at the fringe of an open-air market. A dialogue between two men. The congregation eavesdrops on the conversation.

Props: Two tall stools about six feet apart at stage center, front. They are of sufficient height so that the actors, when seated, are clearly visible to all in the audience.

Two music stands to hold each script, at a height unobtrusive to the audience.

Two headpiece or standing microphones, one for each actor.

Texts: Acts 2:1-11; Romans 8:14-17, 22-27; John 7:37-39.

Adaptation: *Modify all underscored dialogue to adapt to local context.*

'Nudge' card: A sample 'nudge' card appears at the end of this dialogue. Distribute cards before the start of worship. As worship comes to a close, offer a community prayer that the Holy Spirit will nudge the hearts of all gathered. Conclude by asking each person to complete a card; collect the cards as they depart.

.

[**Peter** enters alone, carrying a coffee mug in one hand and what appears to be a newspaper (no front page, no identifying banner) under the other arm. He makes his way casually to a stool, sipping his coffee. He sits and slowly begins leafing through the newspaper until an article catches his attention. He is immersed in reading, oblivious to the space around him. He sits alone for 10-15 seconds, quietly engrossed in reading the paper.

After Peter has been alone, reading for those 10-15 seconds …

Paul enters from the back. He meanders through the milling crowd of the open-air market, peering as though searching for someone. After 10-15 seconds of wandering, he spies Peter from afar … and begins purposefully to make his way to the front.

Peter is unobservant, engrossed in his reading. Paul approaches slowly, uncertain whether the man is, indeed, Peter. Peter remains absorbed in the newspaper, unaware of Paul's approach.]

Paul [clearing his throat … then softly …]: *Peter?*

[Peter is unresponsive, focused on the paper.]

Paul [louder]: *Peter, is that you?*

Peter [looks up and eyes Paul for a moment, then recognizes him]:

Paul? My gosh, it is you … Paul!

[He stands quickly … they embrace enthusiastically.]

Paul:
Ah, Pete … I wasn't sure that was you! Where's your beard? I've never seen you without one.

Peter:
It's spring! I shave every spring, to stand the summer heat. And besides, my mother-in-law likes me better this way … though not today.

What are you doing here? And how did you find me?

[Paul grabs the other stool and pulls it closer ... and both sit.]

Paul:
Well ... I'm here, because I've been looking for you. Your wife said you left in a huff this morning ... said you might be at the market. Why are you here and not out on the boat? Is everything ok?

Peter:
Oh, yeah ... everything's fine. It's just that when I'm home for a while, that house gets kinda small. I love my wife and miss her when I'm gone. And most of the time, I love her mom.

But there are times ...   [Peter rolls his eyes ... they both laugh. Peter continues ...]

It's taken me a long time to learn to just shut my mouth and take a break when the conversation heats up ... so here I am. Two bold women and an ornery old fisherman under the same roof can take its toll. So ... break time!!

But then, you wouldn't understand ... you being a crotchety old bachelor!

[Laughter, both]

Paul:
Yeah ... we both seem to have plenty of ornery in us. Most folks would call it stubborn. Seems God has given each of us a healthy portion of it. Even my young friend, Timothy, called me stiff-necked the other day. Darn kid ... no respect!

[Peter chuckles. Paul continues ...]

In fact, it's Timothy that brings me here. I spent a few days with him last month. He got a letter from a church far away ... past the Great Sea of the West, in <u>a land they call Teh-nah'-see, near the Mountains of Smoke</u>. I wondered whether you've heard of it.

Peter:
Teh-nah'-see? Mountains of Smoke? No, I don't know it. Why the letter?

Paul:
It seems the church is planning a celebration later this year ... during the winter solstice ... and they'd like me to join them. According to the letter, the name of the church is 'St. Paul Evangelical'.

Peter, chuckling:
Well aren't you special? A church named after you! I'll bet your ornery kicked in when you heard that!

Paul:
Yeah ... poor Timothy. He had to put up with my tirade. I'm learning to live with it, I guess ... kinda like you and your mother-in-law!

Peter:
Eh, let's leave the family out of it.

[Pause] *So how far away is it, and when do you leave?*

Paul:
I don't know how far ... and I'm not sure whether I should go, or whether somebody else. I told Timothy I'd get back to him after talking with a few folks. But while with Timothy, he reminded me of a letter I'd written some time ago ... where I encouraged him to 'fan into flame the gift of God that is within him' ... the same gift that is within you and me. The gift of the Spirit.

Peter:
Yeah, Paul ... Timothy showed me that letter during one of his visits a few years ago. I like the way you said it ... that we've been given a Spirit 'not of timidity ... but of power, and of love, and of self-discipline'.

"*Fan into flame ...*' [Peter pauses, thoughtful, staring off into the audience] ...*Claim the Flame ...* [another pause as his gaze slowly returns to Paul] ...

You know, back during the three years when we were with Jesus every day, he taught us a lot of things. Looking back on them, they make sense now. But at the time, I usually didn't get it. He talked about the power of love ... about the power of faith to move mountains ... about trusting in God, and trusting in him ... and not being afraid.

Like the night I got out of the boat to walk on the water, and then fear overtook me and he had to pull me up. "You of little faith," he said. "Why did you doubt?" [Pause ... reflect ... then Peter continues]

'Fan into flame ...' [he says slowly, with remorse ...]

[...and then again, slowly, softly ...] *'Fan into flame ... '*

[Peter pauses, again reflecting. Before he can continue, Paul speaks ...].

Paul:
Ahhh, Peter ... that's been years ago. We've both learned to trust in the power of the Spirit since those days. The Lord saw fit to shake me up on that road to Damascus.

You know, I've often wondered. What was it like for you that day, during the celebration of the wheat harvest ... when the Spirit overpowered you? I've heard others tell the story, how suddenly all you Galileans were speaking in different languages. Do you remember?

Peter:
Oh, yeah. Pentecost. The day that Jesus made good on his promise. Many times since then, we've laughed about it. On that night, after we realized what had happened, we couldn't stop laughing when Phillip observed, 'You know, guys, we ain't in Galilee anymore!'

Folks who were there said it was like a whirlwind. It was a whirlwind! A whirlwind that never ends.

I don't have to tell you, Paul. You've been in that whirlwind ever since you believed. Everybody who believes is in the whirlwind. That's the kind of power you wrote about to Timothy. The kind of power that lifts you up and changes you ... changes your life. The kind of power that brings purpose, meaning.

God breathes that power, the Spirit, into every believer.

Paul:
Amen! Preach it, brother! Over and over, I've had to remind people to 'fan into flame' that gift within them. For the folks at Corinth, and in Ephesus, and in Galatia ... even, probably, for the folks in the church <u>near the Mountains of Smoke</u>. That Jesus' promise of that gift is for everyone ... in just the right way, in just the right amount, for just the right time.

[Paul pauses ... and studies Peter thoughtfully. Then, continuing ...]

You know, Peter ... I can't help but wonder whether you should be the one to go to this <u>land of Teh-nah'-see</u>, not me. Like you said, I'm not sure a 'crotchety old bachelor' is what they need ... or what they deserve!

Peter [thinks a moment, then continues]:
Oh, I don't think so. Long ago, you and I heeded the Spirit's leading. We agreed that I would continue to spread the news about Jesus 'the Christ' to the people of Israel. And you would be the one to proclaim 'the Christ' to the Gentiles. Why God put that into our minds is still a mystery to me. After all, you were the learn-ed Pharisee who knows the Torah backwards and forwards. And me, a simple fisherman from Galilee.

If it had been up to us, clearly we would have decided that you would take 'the Christ' to the Jews, and I would tell the Good News to the Gentiles and the common folk.

But, as scripture says,

> *"For your ways are not my ways", says the Lord.'*

Thinking back on it that was just one more example of how God works. God always works through people where they are, in the circumstances they are in. And it is never a matter of being ready, or being prepared. God takes care of all of that.

Remember back then? At the time, we were confounded. You, the devout Jew. Me, the simple fisherman. But look at the results. You have taken 'the Christ' to places and people I would never have imagined ... thanks be to God.

Paul:
I suppose you're right ... you shouldn't go. But I'm not sure I should, either. [Pause ... thinking. Continuing ...]

But, Peter ... if you did go, what would you say to them? What if the people here in this marketplace [he sweeps his arm across the congregation] *were the Church in <u>the land of Teh-nah'-see</u>? What would you say to them?*

[Peter rises slowly and looks intently at Paul. Then he slowly turns, facing the congregation, and scans his gaze back and forth, just over their heads ... with a distant look in his eyes].

Peter:
Oh, there is probably much I would have to say. I've never been accused of being shy. But something like what you said a moment ago would be part of it:

> *'That Jesus' promise of the gift of the Spirit is for each one of them ...*
> *in just the right way, in just the right amount, for just the right time.'*

And I would proclaim that 'just the right time' is <u>now</u>! <u>In</u> this moment. <u>At</u> this moment. In <u>every</u> moment.

I would probably talk about the timidity you wrote about, in your letter to Timothy. That it is really just fear ... fear of trusting the Spirit at this moment. Of cautioning them against letting timidity have its way ... of always postponing action 'until the Spirit moves me'. Instead, that in trusting that because the gift is within them ... the waiting is over. The Spirit has <u>already</u> moved them!

We both know, Paul, the power of the Spirit. Through the years we've seen that power in countless believers. We've seen that, when believers trust the 'nudge' of the Spirit in their lives, when they claim it and step forward boldly, they begin to experience the future God has planned for them, the future that God desires for them. And when they trust that 'nudge' ... well, then the flame explodes, and so does the church. When each believer fans into flame that gift within them, the future is far beyond their ... beyond our ... imagining.

So I would say to the folks at <u>St. Paul Evangelical</u> ...

> Trust the nudge of the Spirit and its power.
> Trust that Power, to shape the future of their lives ...
> and to shape the future of God's church in <u>the land of Teh-nah'-see near the Mountains of Smoke</u>.

I would also let them know that believers across the Great Sea of the West are praying for them ... and I would ask them to pray for us and all the believers who are far from them, too.

[Peter sits.]

But then ... since I'm not going, they'll never hear what I might have said.

Paul:
Well, I don't know. If there is one thing I've learned since that experience on the road to Damascus, Jesus always gets his way. If the folks at <u>St. Paul Evangelical church</u> are meant to hear your words, they probably will.

But I've gotta go. Somebody said that Luke is in the area, and I want to try to catch up with him before he leaves. I hear he's been talking to a lot of people.

Peter:
Oh, yeah. He grilled me for quite a while about the Pentecost thing. I think he's writing a book. He says he doesn't know why he's doing it, because he doubts whether anyone will read it. But, I guess you could say he's feeling the 'nudge' ... and acting on it. It seems he is trusting that God will bless the future of his writing. All he knows is, he's put off the 'nudge' as long as he can. He says it has been bothering him for years, so he figured he'd better get at it.

But a warning. Don't be in a hurry when you see him. He's loaded with questions.

Paul:
Well, Luke has always asked a lot of questions. Besides, I want to see him about an ailment that's getting worse. And I'm way too old to start looking for another doctor. I don't have the patience, or the time, to train another one!

Peter:
No, you probably don't ... and besides, you're crotchety.

[Laughter. They both stand ... and Peter continues ...]

God speed on your travels, Paul. I look forward to hearing more about the church in <u>the land of Teh-nah'-see</u>.

May the peace of the Lord be with your Spirit.

Paul:
And also with you, my friend.

[They embrace. Paul turns and walks away. Peter sits, staring after him ... then picks up the newspaper and studies it for a few moments. Shortly, he picks up the cup, tucks the newspaper under his arm ... and casually strolls away.]

Sample 'Nudge' Card:

Fan into flame...

God, through the Holy Spirit, is nudging me to:

_____
_____
_____
_____
_____

Name:

_____

Dialogue #3: *The Color Purple*
(Paul and Lydia)

Characters: Paul, the biblical apostle, perhaps dressed in a robe resembling the garb of the 1st century church. A bearded, older man.

Lydia, a wealthy textile and apparel merchant. She is stylish, almost regal in bearing … an elegantly-dressed businesswoman whose favorite color, purple, is evident in her attire.

2 female 'extras', in brief appearance as the scene opens … stylishly clad.

Setting: In the front of the worship center. The setting is the showroom of a retail fabric shop in Jerusalem, featuring upper-end textiles and apparel for the discerning woman. A dialogue between the two main characters, as the congregation eavesdrops on the conversation.

Props: Two tall stools about six feet apart at stage center, front. The stools are of sufficient height so that the actors, when seated, are clearly visible to all in the audience.

Two music stands before the stools to hold each script, at a height unobtrusive to the audience.

A display of various textile/fabric materials, draped over rods or small tables … including samples of quilts and needlework perhaps made by members of the congregation.

Two headpiece or standing microphones, one for each actor.

Texts: Acts 16:11-15, 40; Romans 7:15-25a; Matthew 11:16-19, 25-30.

Adaptation: *Modify all underscored dialogue to adapt to local context.*

The scene opens with the two 'extras' browsing through the textile samples, in quiet small talk between them ... occasionally holding up a different swatch to examine. **Lydia** is with them, animatedly pointing out various aspects of each piece of material. The conversation is muffled.

Paul approaches slowly (up the center aisle) and pauses as though peering through a door before opening it. He steps tentatively into the 'showroom' (facing forward, with his back to the congregation), pausing to survey the scene before him. The two shoppers and Lydia, with their backs to him (and the congregation) are immersed in their muffled conversation and unaware of his presence.

Paul [watches the three women for a moment, then impatiently clears his throat]:
Ahem.

[The women are unresponsive, continuing in their conversation, unaware of his presence.]

Paul [clearly impatient, clears his throat a little louder]:
Ahem!

[Still no acknowledgement from the women, who are examining a fabric sample closely and continuing to face away from the audience]

Paul [more loudly, almost impolitely]:
Excuse me! Is this the shop, called 'The Color Purple'?

Lydia half turns ... her eyes still on the two women and the fabric they are holding: *Yes, sir ... it is. I'll be with you in a moment. We're almost done here, aren't we ladies?*

[The women are nodding gratefully to Lydia, acknowledging that they have found what they need. As they are doing so, Lydia slowly turns toward Paul ... and recognizes him]

Paul! My heavens ... Paul?!!! Is that you??

Paul:

Paul, indeed. And you? The voice sounds familiar, but these old eyes aren't serving me well ...

Lydia:

Oh, Paul ... what a surprise! Please [indicating a stool] *... sit. I'll be right with you.*

[Paul sits on a stool ... as Lydia turns to the women]

Ladies, thank you so much for coming in today. This grand-opening has me in a dither! I'll have that royal silk on the next caravan from either the Thyatira or the Philippi shop, with your name on it. It should be here before the leaves start to fall. Goodbye ... and see you then. [The women leave, down the side aisle]

[Lydia strides over to Paul ... he is seated as she approaches ... with her hand outstretched in elegant fashion.]

Paul ... my dear Paul.

[Paul rises and takes her hand in gentleman courtesy]

What a wonderful surprise! Your eyesight may not be as clear, but your voice is still unmistakable. I'm Lydia. Surely you remember me, from Philippi and Thyatira?

Paul:

Lydia? [As he touches her hand to his lips, in a kiss of greeting] *... My dear, dear Lydia ...* [continuing to hold her hand. He is visibly emotional, and using the other hand, softly wipes a tear from his eye]

Lydia:

Ah ... dear, sweet Paul. Ever the gentleman. So kind and caring. A tent maker, a citizen of the empire, a proclaimer of the Christ ... but ever a gentleman.

[They pause and gaze into each other's eyes]

What brings you here? And how did you learn of 'The Color Purple'? We just opened!

Paul:
Oh, I'm looking for tent liners for my next project ... and someone said there was a new fabric store in Jerusalem. It took me a while to find it! You need to put up a sign!

Lydia:
Yes ... next week. Your old friend, Silas, is making it for me! He's been helping me since I arrived a couple months ago, getting the shop ready. He is such a good man. Ever since meeting him in Philippi, he has been a dear friend.

Paul:
Well, I'm not surprised. He remembers your kindness, for taking us into your summer home and tending us after those terrible beatings.

[His cadence slows, as he remembers the past]

You ... your family ... and all the believers in Philippi ... well, we continue to give thanks to God for them ... and for you.

Lydia:
No, Paul ... it is we who give thanks! You changed my life ... my family's life ... that day at the river, when you and Silas and Timothy told us about 'the Christ', and then baptized all of us. Nothing was the same after that! That church continues to grow ... and the one near our home in Thyatira, too ... with the help of all the believers in Antioch and Ephesus ... even here in Jerusalem.

But why are you in Jerusalem? The last I heard, you were going to Rome, for an audience with Caesar. So much for the rumor mill!

Paul:
No ... that rumor is true. I'm to appear before Caesar late next year.

I've been in Jerusalem to spend some time with Peter and some of the apostles, and with Timothy ... mostly about a church across the Great Sea of the West, <u>near the Mountains of Smoke in a land they call Teh-nah'-see</u>. And rumor has it that Luke will be here in a couple weeks, so I'll spend a few days with him, too. And then there's always tent making, no matter where I go.

Lydia:
<u>Teh-nah'-see ... near the Mountains of Smoke</u>? *How curious ...* <u>'Mountains of Smoke'</u> ... [as she turns toward the fabric display]

Very curious. Here, let me show you something. [She walks over to the display and picks up a couple samples ...]

Last fall, Jah-meel' stopped by my shop in Philippi. Jah-meel' is a wealthy sea captain who travels the world. He has been a loyal customer for many years, and he brings me things from his travels. He told me about a weaver ... well, actually, a quilt maker ... from <u>a land 'near the Mountains of Smoke'</u>. *A church there* <u>... in fact, he said it is called 'St. Paul Evangelical Church'</u> ... *is known for its ministry to the community. Some of Jah-meel's crew were sick ... and the weaver gave him some quilts and blankets made by the women of the church. I guess they give them away ... to homeless people who stay at the church, and to soldiers ... to anybody who has need.*

These aren't for sale ... but I use them to show people how 'the Christ' can change their lives when they become believers.

Paul [looking at the quilts/blankets]:
These are beautiful ... and it sounds like it must be the same church. <u>At least, I hope there aren't more churches near the Mountains of Smoke using my name. One is too many!!</u>

Lydia (chuckling):
<u>Ahh, Paul ... just like you. Your ornery is kicking in!</u>

Paul (chuckles too):
<u>'Ornery'? That's odd, Lydia. A few weeks ago, Peter called me ornery, too. And 'crotchety'. But you're right. Every once in a while, it seems to kick in. I guess it's 'ornery' that gets me in trouble.</u>

Hmmm .... You'd appreciate this. You know that I often write letters to encourage folks ...

Lydia:

Oh, yes! When your letter came to Philippi, we couldn't put it down. We read it over and over. I don't know where it ended up ...

Paul:

Well, I'm in the middle of writing one to the believers in Rome, and my thoughts have been turning to the part of me that you and Peter call 'ornery'. It's a confession, I guess. Sometimes I just don't understand my actions, because I don't do the things I want to do. Instead, I do the very things I hate. I've been trying to figure out why I behave like that.

Lydia:

Oh, Paul ... do I know what you mean! Remember my husband, Aaron?

Paul:

Of course! He was so excited at the baptisms ...

Lydia:

Well ... he's not so excited these days. I said some terrible things before I left ... things I never should have said. They were wrong, and hurtful ... and the worst part, I said them on purpose to make him hurt. Terrible things.

He stayed behind in Thyatira to tend to our store there, and told me to take my time coming home. I feel awful. I've written him two letters ... but I haven't heard from him. I know he's hurt ... and upset.

Yes, I know I'm headstrong ... it's part of who I am. Maybe that's my 'ornery' ...

Paul:

Headstrong. Ornery. Crotchety. All the same, I suppose.

You and I are a lot alike, Lydia. Any man has to be headstrong, sure of his convictions, to be successful in business. And you ... doubly so ... as a woman in a man's world. I recall how proud Aaron was of you and your success.

Lydia:
Oh, yes ... he has been my strongest champion in the business. Any ordinary man would be threatened by my success ... but not Aaron. And that makes even more painful the hurt I have caused.

Paul:
Remember back to that day at the river, Lydia, when you and your family were baptized? How the Holy Spirit came upon you? It was the Holy Spirit that changed you ... not me, not Silas, not Timothy. That was God's hand at work, not ours.

We sometimes forget the power of that Spirit. It was just a couple months ago that Timothy reminded me of something I'd written to him ... to 'fan into flame the gift of God that is within you ...'

On that Sabbath morning at the river, there wasn't any timidity in the air. The power of the Spirit was all around us.

Some people need a kick in the pants so that timidity doesn't have its way. Not you. The power of the Spirit is evident in your life.

But I know I need to sometimes be reminded that it is also a Spirit of love, and of self-discipline. Love, and self-discipline.

Maybe the pain you are feeling around Aaron is a reminder ... to fan into flame the self-discipline of the Spirit. And maybe the pain you're feeling is a reminder for me, too.

Lydia:
Yes ... maybe so. I know the love is there. But maybe I need to reclaim the 'self-discipline' nature of the Spirit. Certainly, to trust it. To live into it.

[She pauses ... and reflects ... and then continues]

I must tell you, though, Paul ... having Silas here has been a real blessing. He has told me about the days when he was with the Jesus crowd ... long before he met you. I guess he didn't spend as much time with Jesus as the Twelve did ... but when he did, it was powerful.

Silas knows how much this thing with Aaron has been weighing on me ... knowing how much I hurt the person I love. And I've told Aaron how much I love him, how sorry I am ... but his silence is hard.

[Another pause ... reflecting]

The other day, Silas shared something Jesus said:

> *'Come to me, all you who are weary and burdened, and I will give you rest. Take my yoke upon you and learn from me, for I am gentle and humble in heart, and you will find rest for your souls.'*

Just the words were soothing. And so, I wait ...

Paul:
I guess for now, Lydia, that's about all you can do. Wait. And give thanks for the love that you have for Aaron, and the love he has for you.

In the meantime, you've given me more to think about for my letter. When I'm at my worst, who will rescue me from my wretchedness? Where will I find rest for my soul? Silas has given us both a clue. Thanks be to God – through Jesus Christ our Lord!

Lydia:
Thanks be to God, indeed!

Paul:
Well, I must be on my way. Your linens are far too luxurious for my tents, so I'll keep looking.

I will pray for you and Aaron ... and trust that God will give you peace. Remember me to Silas.

Lydia:
I will, Paul ... and I will pray for you.

[She extends her hand ... and he returns the gentlemen's kiss. Paul leaves down the center aisle ... as Lydia tends to her wares.]

Dialogue #4: *Doctor's Diagnosis*
(Paul and Luke)

Characters: Paul, the biblical apostle, perhaps dressed in a robe resembling the garb of the 1st century church. A bearded, older man.

Luke, a learned, professional-appearing man ... perhaps wearing a physician's smock or jacket over casual clothes. Sandals. (Ideally, the actor portraying Luke is a real-life healthcare practitioner ... perhaps a doctor or nurse ... familiar with rudimentary physical examination of a medical condition.)

Setting: In the front of the worship center ... seemingly the entry parlor of a 1st century doctor's home which also serves as an examination room. A dialogue between the two main characters, as the congregation eavesdrops on the conversation.

Props: Two tall stools about six feet apart at stage center, front. The stools are of sufficient height so that the actors, when seated, are clearly visible to all in the audience.

Three music stands ... two, before the stools to hold each script, at a height unobtrusive to the audience. The third music stand (or a small table) to the side of Luke's stool ... on which rest a towel, a cup of popsicle sticks, a couple of one-foot square pieces of white cotton (easily torn for bandages), and any other paraphernalia which may be present in the exam room of a 1st century doctor.

A mixing bowl with stirring spoon, along with measuring cup, smaller bowls and medicine bottles are atop the communion rail or small table ... and a bowl containing a handful of dried bay or eucalyptus leaves.

Two headpiece or standing microphones, one for each actor.

Texts: 2 Corinthians 12:7-10; Romans 9:1-5; Matthew 14:13-21.

Adaptation: <u>*Modify all underscored dialogue to adapt to local context.*</u>

As the scene opens, **Luke** is alone and front left ... seemingly absorbed in mixing a potion in a bowl on the communion rail or small table, with his back to the congregation. He is studying recipe notes ... and mixing imaginary ingredients from the several bowls or bottles present.

Paul approaches with confidence up the center aisle, but with a noticeable limp. He pauses to peer through the parlor doorway ... and watches for a few moments. Luke continues to mix his potion, unaware of someone behind him.

After some time, the dialogue begins.

Paul [loudly]:
Hey, you old potion peddler. You got anything that will cure what's wrong with me?

Luke [not turning while continuing to mix his potion ... but clearly recognizing Paul's voice. He responds slowly, while measuring the last ingredient and mixing the bowl. His back is still to Paul and the congregation. He speaks slowly]:

You old, worn out gum flapper! Even Hippocrates couldn't cure what's wrong with you! You've been sick since the day I met you, you broken-down tent maker.

[He wipes his hands on the towel ... and strides over and embraces Paul.]

Ah, Paul ... Timothy told me you'd be stopping by. [The embrace ends, and Luke takes a step back]

He said you're ornier than ever ... something about that persistent thorn in your side. We both laughed. I get quite a kick out of young Timothy. And you know, he cares so deeply about you ... and is very concerned for your health. He said you look 20 years older!

[He pauses to size up Paul]

Good heavens! He's right! What's going on? It's only been a year since you sent me on my way ... but it looks like you've aged 10! Let me take a look at you ...

[He shows Paul to a stool ... and begins to examine his back, shoulders, neck, arms.]

Paul [while Luke is examining]:
I don't know, Luke. You know the terrible pain I've had through the years. It used to come and go. I told the believers in Corinth that it was a messenger from Satan who was sent to torment me ... to keep me from getting conceited about the revelations I'd had. Three times I pleaded with the Lord to take it away from me ... but He said to me:

> *'My grace is sufficient for you; for my power is made perfect in weakness.'*

And yes, His power is made perfect in weakness. But this thorn is getting worse, and the pain doesn't come and go anymore. It's getting harder to sleep through the night. And now it's settling in my wrists and hands!

[Luke takes Paul's hand and begins examining the forearm, wrist, and fingers ...]

Paul [continues]:
Just look how crooked these fingers are!

I can put up with the aches in the legs. But shaping the leather, and sewing the tents? I can still work with the awl ok ... but it's almost to where I can't hold the leather needles ... and I've given up sewing the tent liners. A seamstress is doing that for me.

Luke [continuing to examine throughout this part of the dialogue ... shoulders, raising and lowering the arm, and back to the fingers]:

Well, I'm going to push and pull on your arms for a bit ... so bear with me.

By the way ... Timothy said you're going on a trip across the Great Sea of the West ... to visit a church <u>near the Mountains of Smoke? Something about a winter solstice celebration for sixty years of ministry ... in the land they call 'Teh-nah'-see'?</u>

<u>'St. Paul's Evangelical Church', he said. St. Paul's church, huh?</u> [Luke chuckles noticeably]

Paul:
Don't get me started, Luke. Don't get me started. Just mix me a potion!

Luke:
Ehhh, alright. But I couldn't help myself. A church named for you!

[Luke seems to have finished his examining … and begins tearing narrow strips of cloth (about ½" wide) from the one-foot-square cotton cloth.]

Paul:
Well, I'm not sure I'm gonna make that trip. I think I only have one long trip left in me, and I'm already committed to the audience with Caesar in Rome late next year. Do you remember? You agreed to go with me, Luke … and you know how much it means when you're along … not just to me, but to all the believers along the way. Remember?

Luke:
Yes, I remember … and don't worry, I'll be with you. But based on what I see today, you shouldn't be going anywhere for a while. I've seen you recover from the worst imaginable things … but this body won't endure a long voyage now. It's wearing out. You need to build up your reserve for the trip to Rome, and the time there. We both know that there will be jail time ahead, and if you're to survive the chains in a Roman prison … well, no long trips.

[Luke takes one of Paul's hands …]

I'm going to do something for the most disfigured fingers; I'll explain when I'm done.

[For much of the rest of the dialogue, using the cloth strips and popsicle sticks, Luke wraps a splint around several individual fingers on each hand … continuing until near the end of the skit]

By the way, do you remember Theophilus, the proconsul of the Roman governor at Ephesus? I heard of his large gift to the church there, so I stopped to see him after you left, and ended up staying in his home for a week. He thirsts for 'the Christ'. And I made him a promise … to write down everything I could learn about Jesus 'the Christ' from people who knew Him … and send the finished book to him.

Remember how you encouraged Timothy to 'fan into flame the gift of God that is within you'? That gift, you said, is the Spirit ... not a spirit of timidity ... but a Spirit of power, and of love, and of self-discipline.

Gathering the testimonies of these personal witnesses to Jesus, and seeing the real presence of that Spirit in their lives ... well, this book has become my life purpose, my 'Claim the Flame' purpose. I don't know what Theophilus will do with it when it's done, but listening to these stories has been powerful!

In fact, last week I tracked down a member of the royal court of Queen Candace, from Ethiopia. His business in Jerusalem will conclude by the new moon, when he expects to depart. He was asking about you. I hope you can find time to see him before you both leave.

Paul:
Well, maybe so. I want to spend a little time with Timothy's mother, Eunice, before I head back to Tarsus and some rest. And I've promised to sit down with Timothy again so we can settle who should go to the celebration with the believers in <u>Teh-nah'-see ... near the Mountains of Smoke</u>.

Luke:
You know, Paul, during our many travels together we saw miracles and we endured hardship. But you, especially ... all the terrible beatings. And the most severe ones came from your brothers, the children of Abraham. And now, from all the testimonies I've heard, it was the same with Jesus. The most severe punishment came from the temple priests and teachers of the Torah, teachers of the Mosaic laws.

Even you ... before Jesus turned your life upside down on that trip to Damascus. Before then, you were one of the cruelest to the Jesus followers. I think that is what has Theophilus so confused ... and why it is so important to collect the stories from people who walked with Jesus and knew Him.

Paul:
Yeah, well ... you've heard my 'Jesus story' so many times, you're probably sick of it. That 'old' me, died on the Damascus road. 'The Christ' raised me to new life.

My heart weeps for the children of Abraham ... my brothers and sisters. Since His promise to Abraham, God has blessed them ... with teachers, and prophets, and guidelines for living ... and now, through 'the Christ'. But they remain stiff-necked people. I know ... I was one of them.

Even so ... if I could trade my life for theirs so they would know Jesus ... I would, and overflow with joy. But no ... their ears are stopped ... their eyes don't see. And my heart weeps.

Luke:
Yes, I know how much it grieves you. Your eloquence is lost to them.

Oh ... something else happened a couple weeks ago. Thaddeus, one of the Twelve, took me to the synagogue where one of the scribes is a believer. The scribe read from the scroll of Isaiah:

> *"Come, all you who are thirsty, come to the water; and you who have no money, come, buy and eat! ... Listen to me, and eat what is good, and your soul will delight in the richest fare. Give ear and come to me; hear me that your soul may live."*

Then Thaddeus told us about the day when, with just five loaves of bread and two fish, all the people in the crowd were fed. "You can't imagine it," he said. "Thousands of people, sitting quietly and eating until they were satisfied ... and enough left over for us, too!"

I guess that a few weeks before then, Jesus had been telling them to stop worrying about worldly things, like where they would get food or clothes. He just kept inviting people to 'come and drink, come and eat'. Judas was always complaining because they were running out of money. Herod had just beheaded John the Baptizer ... which really scared them! But Jesus said not to worry. And then, that day, thousands of people with no food and they with no money. All of a sudden, baskets overflowing! "We were shocked!" Thaddeus said. It took them a long time to really believe that, as Peter said, "You are 'the Christ', the Son of the living God."
[Luke pauses ... lifting up one of Paul's hands and admiring his splint handiwork]

Almost done, here.

[He starts tidying up his work table, and eventually turns to Paul with three dried leaves]

Paul:
You know, Luke ... as the years have gone by, I've learned a few things. There are times to proclaim, and times for a soft touch ... so that at the name of Jesus, every knee should bow, and every tongue confess that Jesus is Lord.

When Jesus comes into your heart, you are changed. The old dies, and new life begins. And we never know when that is going to happen, but it does. For some, it begins with a gentle but persistent nudge. For stubborn folks like me, it takes a pretty hard whack. But from that moment on, as believers ... as followers ... it gets easier and easier to tell the story, thanks be to God.

And we must tell the story, each one of us. The story of this Jesus, the name above all names. The world is waiting to hear.

Luke:
Amen, brother. Preach it!

Paul [holding up his splinted fingers and staring at them]:
So, what's going on here? What have you done?

Luke:
Well, it seems you have a condition the Greeks call ... 'arthro', which means 'joint' ... 'itis', which means 'inflammation'. Arthro-itis. Joint inflammation.

In plain Aramaic, you have swollen joints. It is usually caused by a trauma to the joint, and made worse with old age. Heaven knows, your joints have seen plenty of trauma ... and you aren't getting any younger!

There are two things for the best treatment: Rest ... and keep the joints from moving with braces or splints. A doctor friend says he's had some success with herbal treatments, too.

So ...

1. *Keep the splints on for three days ... then off for three days ... back on for three ... and keep repeating;*
2. *Here are some dried eucalyptus leaves. Go over to Samuel's Apothecary and get a month's supply. Grind up three a day and sprinkle them on your food.*
3. *Rest ... get three more hours of sleep every day.*

Remember ... take three leaves a day ... and get plenty of rest. And come back and see me in three weeks.

Paul [clearly exasperated]:
Whoa, Doc ... you've got a bad case of the 'threes', here! Three on, three off ... three leaves a day ... three more hours of sleep. And how am I going to get any sleep with these sticks on my hands anyway, never mind make tents?

Luke [returning to his mixing bowls and away from Paul]:
Ahhh ... go! I'll see you in three weeks ...

[Luke tends to the mixing bowls and his recipe]

Paul [stands in disbelief, then slowly leaves the parlor and begins walking down the center aisle ... hands held at eye level for the audience to clearly see, staring at his hands ... and mutters loud enough for Luke to hear]:

Take three a day, and get plenty of rest. What is the world coming to?

[Paul exits.

After a few moments, exit **Luke**.]

Dialogue #5: *Doubt*
(Paul and the Ethiopian eunuch)

Characters: Paul, the biblical apostle, perhaps dressed in a robe resembling the garb of the 1st century church. A bearded older man.

Ethiopian eunuch, the senior attendant to the court of the Ethiopian queen. He is refined with a regal bearing, wearing finely tailored casual clothes with a silk ascot or scarf. Ideally, the actor is of African descent.

Setting: In the front of the worship center. At an open air market, an informal gathering place for casual conversation in 1st century Jerusalem. A dialogue between the two main characters, as the congregation eavesdrops on the conversation.

Props: Two tall stools at stage center, front. The stools are of sufficient height so that the actors, when seated, are clearly visible to all in the audience.

Three music stands. Two of the stands, one in front of each stool, hold the actors' scripts ... at a height unobtrusive to the audience. The third stand serves as a side table to one of the stools.

A newspaper and coffee mug.

Two headpiece or standing microphones, one for each actor.

Texts: Acts 8:26-39; Romans 13:8-14; Matthew 18:15-20.

Adaptation: <u>Modify all underscored dialogue to adapt to local context.</u>

As the scene opens, **Paul** is seated on a stool, casually reading the newspaper and sipping coffee … oblivious to the marketplace bustle.

The **Ethiopian eunuch** (i.e., **Ee**) approaches slowly along a side aisle … pausing occasionally to survey the marketplace crowd. He is looking for someone. As he nears the front of the aisle, he spies Paul, who is inattentive. He approaches Paul slowly and respectfully from the side … and stands quietly, looking at him patiently.

Paul is engrossed in the newspaper, and on turning a page notices **Ee** out of the corner of his eye. He pauses to size up the stranger, still holding the newspaper. **Ee** is looking at **Paul** directly, remaining respectfully silent.

Paul [opens the dialogue]:
Yes?

Ee [deferentially]:
Pardon me, sir. But I am told that you are Paul of Tarsus. Is that so?

Paul:
I am Paul of Tarsus. Who is asking?

Ee:
Begging your pardon, sir. Forgive me for interrupting you here, but I was hoping to find you this morning. Luke told me that you often begin your day at the marketplace. I am so glad to have found you at last.

My name is unimportant. For many years I have been privileged to serve her majesty the queen of Ethiopia as her personal attendant. My royal duties in Jerusalem were concluded yesterday, so I will return tomorrow. On finding you at last, my visit and my joy is now complete. Thanks be to God!

Paul [setting the newspaper and mug aside]:
Ah … yes. Luke had mentioned that you were in Jerusalem. He shared a little of his conversation with you … and how your life was changed some years ago on another return trip. It was an encounter with Phillip, as I recall. Luke said you hoped to find me.

[Paul gestures toward the empty stool, and Ee sits as the dialogue continues]

Why? How could I be of help in your service to the Queen?

Ee:
Yes, it was on the road to Gaza. I will never forget. I was in the carriage, reading the words of the prophet. A stranger asked the driver to stop ... and he entered and sat alongside. His name was, indeed, Phillip ... and he began to explain Isaiah's prophecy. He told of what had happened a few days before ... about Jesus and His crucifixion ... his resurrection ... of Jesus as 'the Christ', the promised Messiah.

He talked of new life, of baptism. I asked if this 'new life' was meant for me, too. So we stopped at a pond. Phillip prayed that the Spirit would come ... and then he baptized me. At that instant, everything changed. I cannot explain it, but my life changed. When I told Luke, he wrote it all down. He told me about his journeys with you, and the Spirit changing people's lives. Later, I talked with Timothy. And then I prayed that I might find you.

Paul:
When Luke mentioned you, I recalled that I had heard of your story ... and now I remember where. A few months ago while on my return to Jerusalem, I stopped in Caesarea and stayed with Phillip in his home for a few days. He described your encounter with the Spirit on that road to Gaza. The more he shared, the more it became apparent to me that your experience happened at the same time my life was being turned upside down on the road to Damascus. So, my friend, it seems we share a common 'rebirth' as brothers ... and a common destiny in this new life in Jesus, the Christ.

Ee:
Forgive me, sir. But it was after talking with Timothy that it became important for me to find you. Because while we may share a common rebirth in this new life, I fear that we do not share 'a common destiny', to use your words. And I am afraid.

Paul:
Afraid? Afraid of what?

Ee:
From Luke and Timothy, and from many others, it seems this 'new life' has been exploding all around the empire ... exploding because believers get so excited that they can't help but share the 'good news' of the Christ. And Timothy said you will soon travel far away .... across the Great Sea of the West to <u>a land they call Tehnah'–see, near the Mountains of Smoke</u> ... to celebrate how the Spirit is at work there, too. Believers in the grip of the Spirit ... excited believers, in every nation!

Paul:
Yes, when the Spirit comes, things happen. We can both testify to that.

Ee:
Yes, that is true. Your wisdom in the Spirit is well known, as are your journeys to Galatia, through Asia, and across Macedonia. Believers in Egypt speak of you, even in my home city in Ethiopia. And some of my Coptic brothers in church speak of stories of your travels.

But lately, one of the brothers has caused problems. He speaks unkindly of another brother. He complains of our time together in prayer. Some no longer come, because of the tension. I have tried to talk with him, but I am a humble man. He sneers when I approach. It is hurtful.

Paul:
Yes, I have seen this before. It is the work of Satan. The devil starts small and uses little things to cause schism in a church. And before they realize it, the community has become numb to it. Soon, love of neighbor gives way to jealousy and dissension. The community loses sight of its foundation ... of 'the Christ'. You and your brothers must come back to that foundation.

Ee:
We have tried. But this man's presence and influence are great. When we turn to Scripture, or call for prayer, he is disruptive. We struggle with 'love your neighbor', because he is our neighbor, too.

Paul:
These are difficult matters. Moses reminds us that 'love your neighbor' has been God's will for humanity from the beginning. I've listened to Peter and James tell how

Jesus embraced this teaching of the prophets. 'Love God, and love your neighbor', He said. It sounds so simple.

But Jesus is wise to the ways of men when Satan intervenes, and so his insight on sin is helpful in times like these. Jesus knows our weakness. Peter remembered his words clearly, and told me that he has used the teaching himself. Jesus said to them,

> 'If any member of the church sins against you, go and point out the fault when the two of you are alone. If he listens, you have regained him. But if he does not listen, take one or two others along with you, so that every word can be confirmed by someone else. If he still does not listen, take it to the whole church. If his heart does not change, treat him as one outside the church.'

And pray. Jesus promises to be present. But if a brother refuses to change, then 'love of neighbor' means love for the rest of the community so that the community remains clothed in Christ.

[Paul takes a long pause, to let his words sink in. Then he continues...]

Was this your fear?

Ee:
Your insight is helpful, Learned One. And this matter has been heavy on my mind. But, no, it is something else which I fear and which has led me to you. It is difficult for me to speak of it.

Paul:
My brother ... what troubles you so?

Ee:
It is difficult for me to speak it. [A long, long pause ...]

It has been twenty years since Phillip baptized me on the road to Gaza. When the Spirit came upon me, it was indescribable. Joy. Peace. Purpose. An overflowing Presence. It gripped me for days. Even as the days turned into months, and into years, it gripped me.

But in recent years ... I feel adrift. And I am afraid. In fact, there are times when I wonder whether there ever really <u>was</u> that overflowing Presence. I have been struggling, not knowing if the Joy, the Peace, and the Purpose I felt that day ... if it was real, or imagined.

And so, my greatest fear: that because of my doubt, the Spirit has left me. That God has left me. That I am alone ... abandoned.

[Another long pause ... as he stares at his feet...]

So, you might ask, 'Why seek out you?'

Paul:
Hmmmm ... that thought <u>has</u> been going through my mind ...

Ee:
It was your young friend, Timothy. Timothy had learned that I was in Jerusalem, and he sought me. He had heard, too, of my 'road to Gaza' experience, and he wanted to hear it from me. I shared how vivid the Spirit was that day, and for years afterward. But when I shared that I was drifting ... no longer sure ... well, he smiled.

'I have had those same feelings,' he said. Then he showed me a letter you had sent him. You knew of his struggle. 'Fan into flame,' you said. 'Fan into flame the gift of God that is within you. For you have been given a Spirit not of timidity ... but of power ... and of love ... and of self-discipline.'

It was Timothy who encouraged me to find you.

Paul:
My dear Timothy. God has blessed me in these many journeys with dear friends. But none as precious as Timothy. He is close to my heart.

Ee:
But why those words, Paul? Why those words to Timothy? What did you see about him that prompted those words?

Paul:

My friend, you must know some things about Timothy, and about me and my love for him, to understand the reasons for that letter. Timothy grew up in Lystra. His father is Greek, and his mother, a Jew. From a small boy, his mother and grandmother were steadfast in raising him according to Jewish teaching. To his father, those teachings were irrelevant.

It was on a return trip through Lystra that we met. From an earlier stay, many had come to believe in 'the Christ' ... including his mother and grandmother. And Timothy. He was earnest in his questions, so Silas and I invited him to come with us. He has been a faithful companion through the years.

Ee:

Yes, the young man is very fond of you. He speaks with deep respect and kindness. But, sir ... why the words in the letter?

Paul:

Ahhh, my impatient friend, yes ... the letter.

I have seen the Spirit come alive in people in many different ways, as no doubt have you. Your encounter on the road to Gaza, and mine on the road to Damascus, were power-filled, and changed our lives in an instant.

Not Timothy. Timothy's path in believing was step-by-step, beginning from earliest memories. For him and for many, it begins with regular teaching as a child ... with him, the teaching came from a mother and a grandmother. He was a young man when we met, and his traditions helped him to grasp the meaning of 'the Christ'. When we laid hands on him and the Spirit filled him, he received the same power which every believer receives in baptism... the power to proclaim how the presence of 'the Christ' in their life is a promise that God intends for everyone.

Timothy is a fine young man, and a committed Christ-follower. But he will tell you that he went through a time where his attention wandered to other things ... things in his life which seemed right and purposeful. His life started down a different path, and he struggled. We talked of his struggles, of what troubled him.

I have learned not to question God. But sometimes I wonder when someone like you or me ... a person who has had a 'road-to-Gaza' or 'road-to-Damascus' experience

... I wonder whether it is possible for us to grasp how difficult it can be for a believer to remain convicted in the faith .. To Claim the Flame ... when the understanding is spoon-fed to them, gradually. That was Timothy's struggle. He never said it, but I think he was questioning whether his faith was as genuine as mine, because he lacked that [Paul emphatically slaps his head] *'slapped-upside-the-head' experience.*

Ee:
I can see why Timothy calls you 'the Learn-ed One'.

Paul:
Well, now you have a deeper insight into the letter to Timothy. But we've not addressed the fear you have, which brought us together. You said that because of your doubt, your greatest fear is that the Spirit has left you. That God has left you. And now you feel alone ... abandoned.

Ee:
Yes ... that is my fear. I am afraid that God has left me.

Paul:
Oh, my friend ... that is a lonely place to be ... when doubt overtakes you. But God has not left you. It is the Spirit within that keeps you searching. It is the Spirit within that has led you to Luke ... to Timothy ... to me. It is the Spirit within that nudges you to community in regular worship, study and prayer.

It is in encouraging one another, and building each other up, that we love God and love neighbor. And through mutual encouragement, we feel God's presence in our lives.

God has not left you, my friend. The Spirit is present, even now. It has never left.

My words of encouragement to you would be the same as to Timothy ... and to believers gathered in every time and place ... whether in Jerusalem, or in Ethiopia, or <u>in the land they call Teh-nah'-see, near the Mountains of Smoke</u>:

> *Fan into flame the gift of God that is within you, for you have been given a Spirit not of timidity ... but of power, and of love, and of self-discipline.'*

So for you, reClaim the Flame. And my instruction for you today would be just as for Timothy at the close of that letter:

'Proclaim the word; be persistent whether it is convenient or inconvenient; convince, reprimand, encourage through all patience and teaching.'

My friend, we have been given the greatest of gifts: the love of God in our lives, in Jesus 'the Christ'. As fellow believers, how can we not share that gift? It is in sharing that we reClaim the Flame!

Ee [rising to stand, with hand extended]:
Thank you, Learn-ed One. Indeed, I now know that God has not left me ... for God has blessed me today through your words.

May you enjoy God's peace.

[Paul takes his hand, and they embrace.]

Paul:
And you, my friend. Safe travels on your journey home. Please greet all the sisters in the court of Her Excellency, the Queen ... and our brothers and sisters in the church which gathers there. You are in the prayers of many.

The Lord be with your spirit. Grace be with you.

[Ee leaves. Paul sits for a moment, gathering his newspaper and mug ... watching as Ee recedes. After a moment, Paul exits.]

Dialogue #6: *Women of Faith*
(Paul and Eunice)

Characters: Paul, the biblical apostle, perhaps dressed in a robe resembling the garb of the 1st century church. A bearded, older man.

Eunice, mother of Timothy. She is dressed in the casual house clothes of a 1st century homemaker.

Setting: In the front of the worship center. The drama takes place in the sitting room of her home in Lystra. A dialogue between the two characters, as the congregation eavesdrops on the conversation.

Props: Two tall stools at stage center, front, separated by a flat music stand (as a serving table). The stools are of sufficient height so that the actors, when seated, are clearly visible to all in the audience.

Three music stands ... one in front of each stool to hold the actors' scripts, at a height unobtrusive to the audience ... and the third located between the stools (as a serving table).

A tea pot and two mugs, at rest on the serving stand.

Two headpiece or standing microphones, one for each actor.

Popsicle sticks and cloth strips (for finger splints).

Texts: Philippians 3:4b-14; Galatians 3:26-28.

Adaptation: <u>*Modify all underscored dialogue to adapt to local context.*</u>

[As the scene opens, the characters are seated on the stools, with the teapot and mugs on the table between. Three of **Paul's** fingers on his dominant hand are in splints.

They are seated so that Paul's dominant hand is easily visible to the audience when he receives the mug (see script) from Eunice ... and remains visible as he occasionally sips his tea throughout.

The dialogue begins.]

Eunice [while pouring tea into the mugs, and handing one to Paul]:
Paul, it is such a pleasure to welcome you into my home again. It has been far too long. Please ... have some tea. Timothy tells me you have developed a fondness for it recently.

Paul:
Thank you, Eunice [as he receives the mug]. *You shouldn't have gone to the bother. I don't expect to stay long, but it is so nice to see you again. And, as always, your home brings me peace.*

[He sips the tea.]

But no ... your son is misled. It isn't the tea that I am fond of. It's what I put in it. Doc Luke has me mixing in dried eucalyptus leaves ... supposed to be three a day. It's not the tastiest potion he's ever come up with. I can't say it's helping very much, but when it comes to medicine, he can be hard to live with, when I don't do what he says. So, just to keep peace between us, I do what he says.

Eunice:
Yes, Timothy has told me about some of Luke's 'cures'. Let me guess ... does that explain your fingers? Is that more of the good Doctor's work?

Paul:
Yes, indeed. Splints on these three fingers [he holds up the splinted fingers for the audience to see] *... three days on, three days off. He thinks the tea and the splints ... and more sleep ... will fix what ails me. I have three more months to go, and then another visit with him.*

I'm not sure there's a cure in all this. I think he's just toying with me ... testing me, to see if I can follow orders. He said something about preparing me for what lies ahead for the trip to Rome in the spring. He knows how hard it is for me to be submissive, especially to Roman authority ... so, I think he's testing me. Making me follow orders.

But he gets far too much pleasure out of watching me put up with this ... [he nods to the splinted fingers ... and both chuckle.]

Eunice:
Well, Luke has been a loyal companion with you, and with my son, Timothy. I remember the terrible beating you endured on your first visit to Lystra ... and it was Luke who nursed you to health. It was a miracle you lived, Paul.

Paul:
Yes, thanks be to God for Luke's healing touch ... and for you, Eunice, and your dear mother, Lois. If you had not opened your home for those weeks and tended to us, I don't know what would have happened. And the whole time, young Timothy peppering Luke and Barnabas with question after question. He was thirsting to learn all he could about Jesus 'the Christ ... probably because you and his grandmother were so faithful from his earliest days in taking him to synagogue and grounding him in Hebrew law and tradition.

It was no surprise on my return a few years later, to learn how much he had grown in the faith. And even more, your strength in the faith ... when you encouraged him to trust the Spirit, to step out in faith, and to come along with Silas and Luke and me.

Eunice: *Yes, I was so proud of him. But by the time you all left, I can tell you now that Mom and I were a little scared.*

Paul:
Scared? Scared of what?

Eunice [pauses to stare at him ... then continues]:
I'll never understand men! 'Scared of what', you ask? Scared of you! And scared of that doctor, Luke!

Paul:
Of Luke and me? Why? Why were you scared of us?

Eunice:
You're a man, Paul. I don't think a man can really understand the fear a mother has when a child leaves home. A man will never know the feel of a baby at a mother's breast. Or the tender caress when a boy hurts. Or the delight in watching him grow as he eats the meals prepared by the loving hands of a mother.

A mother gives her life providing for her children. And as they grow, in preparing them for a future without her. All the while, hoping to have the strength to let go when that time comes, trusting that her adult child will be safe.

His grandmother and I had just entrusted him to your care …

[Paul is slowly sipping his tea … as Eunice continues …]

… And what is the first thing you have Doctor Luke do? He circumcises him, for heaven's sake!

[Paul is caught by surprise and coughs on the tea … while Eunice laughs as Paul recovers]

So … is it any wonder, this mother was a little scared for her boy as you left town?

Paul [smiling, as he puts down the tea and reaches for her hand]:
Well, when you put it that way, I can see why you might have been scared. But I don't think you were anywhere near as scared as Timothy was, when he saw the Doc coming at him with the knife in his hand …

[They both laugh … as Paul continues to hold her hand.]

Paul [continues]:
Well, I guess we really tested his faith, huh? But from the moment Timothy left your home, he has been a deep and true friend. What a blessing; no one is more dear to me.

And so, whenever I think of you, Eunice ... I thank my God [as he releases her hand.]

Eunice:
Well, thank you, Paul. Your words are very kind.

[She pauses to sip her tea ... then continues ...]

But what brings you to Lystra? You have been in Jerusalem, I know ... but Timothy said you were heading back to Tarsus for some rest ... something about getting ready for a long trip ahead, across the Great Sea of the West.

And why stop to see me ... though, of course, you are always welcome here.

[She pours more tea for both of them ...]

Paul [pausing to sip his tea, then continuing]:
Well, Timothy said another letter had come from the church <u>in the land of Teh-nah'-see, near the Mountains of Smoke</u>. Do you have it? Or do you know what it said?

Eunice:
No, I don't have it. In his last letter, Timothy asked me to read it and then send it on to you in Tarsus. A caravan came through last week on its way to Antioch, so I gave it to the guide. By now it is probably at your home. Timothy said he was going to meet you there in the next few weeks during his return from Jerusalem.

Paul:
Were you able to read it? Or your husband? As I recall, he is Greek and knows several languages.

Eunice:
Yes, he read what he could. He thinks it is of the Celtic tongue, not a common language. And a word unfamiliar to him ... 'committee', I think he said. This 'committee' shared some of their plans for <u>the winter solstice</u> celebration. They were excited to get Timothy's reply to their last letter. I guess he shared about your encouragement to him, to 'Fan into flame' the gift of the Spirit that is within them ... and they have chosen that as their theme. Now, they are eager to hear the details of your visit.

Oh yes, one other thing. If my husband interpreted it correctly, it seems their church is named after you ... St. Paul Evangelical Church, I think. My husband was very impressed, and we both laughed ... knowing you! [She chuckles ...]

Paul:
Well, he and I will talk about that later. Timothy got an earful about that when he read me the last letter from the 'committee'. As I have explained many times, it is 'the Christ' whose name we bear. Not mine. Not Apollos. Only Jesus, 'the Christ'. But as I said, we will talk of that some other time.

Do you recall anything else?

Eunice:
Yes.

The celebration will honor their history in this land called Teh-nah'-see, near the Mountains of Smoke. And in honoring their past, they are looking to the future. They have heard of your work in spreading the news of 'the Christ' ... and have even read some of the letters you wrote to the churches in Asia and Thessalonica. They are looking for ways to 'Fan into flame' the gift of the Holy Spirit. They want to trust the Spirit to shape the ministry of their church for the generations ahead.

He said the letter was filled with excitement about your visit. They are eager to see you! When do you leave?

Paul:
I don't know. Timothy and I will talk about that when we meet. I know of no better example of someone who has taken that encouragement to heart ... to 'fan into flame the gift of God that is within you.' Timothy has grown well past the timidity I warned about. He has claimed the flame!

But so many believers struggle with trusting the power of the Spirit ... and the love and the self-discipline that comes with that power. It is timidity that holds them back.

As we have seen all over the empire, Eunice ... even right here in Lystra ... when believers learn to place their trust in the power of the Spirit, 'the Christ' is proclaimed and the church explodes!

Eunice:

Speaking of churches exploding ... Lydia was a guest in my home a few weeks ago. She had spent the summer at her home in Philippi, and was on her way back to her fabric shop in Jerusalem. She was so excited that you had stopped by the shop just before her grand opening. I guess Silas helped her get it up and running.

Paul:

Yes, her shop was a surprise! I was looking for some tent-liners, but she only carries very fine fabrics. Not right for my tents. But it was good to see her. How is she?

Eunice:

She is well. She told me of the strain between her and Aaron, her husband. I guess he wasn't too happy about her launch of the Jerusalem store, and how long she would be away. She had said some things that hurt him. So the summer together was good for them, and she has a spring in her step again. She is very grateful to you, for the kind counsel while you were in her shop. It seems your words helped her get back on track with Aaron.

Paul:

Ahhh that is good news! Like you, years ago Lydia opened her home to me after I had been beaten nearly to death. I am indebted to her for that recovery.

Eunice:

Well, she was talking about a letter you have written to her church in Philippi. They've been sharing it with believers all over Macedonia!

You know, Paul, since Lydia was here, I've been thinking back to that first visit years ago ... and your fiery speeches. It seemed like your zeal in telling about 'the Christ' got you in trouble with everybody ... the Roman governor, the Sadducees and the Pharisees ... even the Greeks, who don't have any religious axe to grind and don't care what god you worship.

Lydia and I were talking about that. Even in your first letter to the church in Corinth, you said some things about women that caused us pain when we first heard it.

'Women should remain silent in churches', you said. 'They are not to speak ... and if they have questions, they should ask their husbands at home.'

Paul:
Well, before you go too far … [but Eunice interrupts while Paul is speaking … stepping on his line …]

Eunice:
No, Paul … I am sorry, and I don't mean to be disrespectful. But let me finish, because this is important to Lydia, and to me and my mom. A few years after that letter to the Corinthian church, you wrote a letter to the churches in our region … to the churches in Galatia. We read that letter over and over, because it was so powerful. It put a different light on things, and I know it by heart. Do you remember? You said to us,

'But now that faith has come, we are no longer subject to a disciplinarian, for in Christ Jesus you are all children of God through faith. As many of you as were baptized into Christ have clothed yourselves with Christ. There is no longer Jew nor Greek, there is no longer slave nor free, there is no longer male and female; for all of you are one in Christ Jesus.' …

[Eunice pauses to take a breath, and Paul jumps in immediately …]

Paul:
You need to understand that … [and again, Eunice interrupts, stepping on Paul's line …]

Eunice:
I'm sorry, Paul … but let me finish.

[Paul leans back … and is silent out of respect, but clearly exasperated. Eunice doesn't wait, but continues …]

Lydia is the one who said it first. We have noticed a change in you, from the early days. Oh, your preaching is as powerful and eloquent as ever. But before, there was an edge to your words. But in your recent letters, and in your presence, there seems to be a softness in your heart. There is an urgency, yes … but a softness.

That urgency, and that softness, comes through in the letter to Lydia's church. You speak of gaining Christ, and growing in righteousness … the righteousness from God based on faith.

'But this one thing I do;' you wrote, 'forgetting what lies behind and straining forward to what lies ahead, I press on toward the goal for the prize of the heavenly call of God in Christ Jesus.'

Maybe you don't notice it, Paul ... but we do. Women of faith see it in you, and it fills us with hope. And in our hope, we, too, press on toward that goal of the heavenly call of God in Christ Jesus. And we give thanks to God for a church we do not yet see, but a church our children, and our children's children, will see.

[There is a long silence. Paul is transfixed. His eyes have softened, no longer exasperated.]

Paul:
You are so very kind, Eunice ... and gracious. I am grateful that you kept pressing forward, and didn't let me interrupt.

I am not sure what lies ahead for me, in Rome. I don't know what the outcome of the trial before Caesar will be. It doesn't matter. But this time of waiting seems to be bringing me closer and closer to 'the Christ' ... a deeper understanding of the mystery of God in 'the Christ'.

Yes ... in my younger days, I was filled with zeal, and my words may have seemed harsh. Maybe I deserved some of those beatings.

But I am certain of this, Eunice. God makes no distinction between male and female. His grace is in equal measure, for all ... no distinction. For this old Pharisee, that has been a hard truth to accept. For I am convinced that nothing will separate you or me, male or female, from the love of God that is in Christ Jesus.

Nothing.

And so, I am grateful for you, Eunice ... and for Lydia ... and for Lois ... as equals in the faith. And as I think about it, for so many others: Priscilla and Dorcas ... Phoebe and Nympha ... so many. No distinction in God's eyes.

Eunice:
Once again, Paul, God has blessed me through you ... as he has blessed Timothy. I will tell Timothy of our time together.

Paul:
Well, I will see him before you do, when he stops by my home in Tarsus in a few weeks. We have promised to settle who will visit the church <u>in Teh-nah'-see, near the Mountains of Smoke</u>. <u>The winter solstice</u> is fast approaching.

[They both stand and approach one another]

Eunice [taking his splinted hand in hers]**:**
Take care of yourself, Paul ... tend to those fingers, and remember your tea. You need to stay on Luke's good side as the trial in Rome gets closer. May God be with you.

[They embrace warmly]

Paul:
And with your spirit, my dear sister. Blessings, and peace.

[Paul departs down the center aisle, as Eunice watches him leave. She departs the side aisle.]

Dialogue #7: *Whom Shall I Send?*
(Paul and Timothy)

Characters: Paul, the biblical apostle, dressed in the garb of the 1st century church. A bearded, older man.

Timothy, Paul's young protégé, dressed similarly. At least a generation younger.

Setting: In the front of the worship center. The drama takes place on the porch of Paul's home in Tarsus. A dialogue between the two characters, as the congregation eavesdrops on the conversation.

Props: Two tall stools at stage center, front. The stools are of sufficient height so that the actors, when seated, are clearly visible to all in the audience.

Two music stands … one in front of each stool to hold the actors' scripts, at a height unobtrusive to the audience.

Two headpiece or standing microphones, one for each actor.

Texts: Genesis 12:1-3; Matthew 5:1-10.

Adaptation: *Modify all underscored dialogue to adapt to local context.*

[As the scene opens, **Paul** is seated on one of the stools. He is staring into the distance, awaiting the arrival of his young friend. **Timothy** slowly enters the back of the sanctuary. Paul, upon seeing him, breaks into a broad smile and waits patiently as Timothy walks casually up the center aisle. At about halfway, as he continues to walk, the dialogue begins.]

Paul [calls out loudly]:
Ah, Timothy. I've been waiting for you ... but I didn't know whether it would be today or tomorrow ...

[Timothy approaches, his back to the audience ... and pauses].

Paul [remains seated and stretches his hand to indicate the empty stool]:
Sit, my young friend. It is so good to see you. How was the journey from Jerusalem?

Timothy [sits and takes Paul's extended hand in his, grasping it gently]:
It is good to see you too, Paul. Even though it's only been a few months, it seems much longer.

[With his other hand, **Timothy** now cradles Paul's hand in both and continues]: *The trip was fine ... but my plans changed. I decided to go visit Mom at home in Lystra and maybe catch up with you there ... but you had left the day before. So I stayed a couple weeks with her and Grandma Lois.*

Mom told me you had splints on your fingers. [He looks more closely at Paul's fingers] *... Looks like Doctor Luke's miracle cures are working. They look fine. Is the pain gone?*

Paul [withdrawing his hand]:
Oh, these are fine ...

[He holds up his hand and flexes the fingers freely for all to see].

Nothing wrong with them. But Luke didn't touch these fingers.

[He holds up the other hand, again for all to see, with the fingers appearing as though very crooked and stiff.]

These are the ones that are giving me fits! And now my knees!

No ... I gave up on Luke's splints and nasty potion a couple weeks ago. I'd rather take my chances with Roman jailers than with his medicine!

[Shared laughter ...]

Timothy:
Well, it's good to be in your home again. What a beautiful morning, out here on the porch. I can see why you return to Tarsus now and then, Paul. When are you going to settle down, and make this your home? Maybe after your trips to Rome and <u>the land they call Teh-nah'-see</u>? Luke says your body is wearing out ... and by the looks of those fingers, I'd say he's right. Maybe you need to listen to him.

Paul:
You're not here to talk about my health, Timothy. And, by the way, your Mom talks too much!

But I do appreciate your making the trip, so we can decide about the visit to the church <u>near the Mountains of Smoke</u> across the Great Sea of the West. Eunice said she had sent the last letter here to my home, but no one knows where it is.

Did you read it? And is my memory right ... that their celebration is planned during <u>the winter solstice</u>? That's soon upon us!

Timothy:
Well, Mom was part right. I had sent parts of the letter so she could ask Dad about some of the language. She was supposed to send it here, along with Dad's notes. But it doesn't matter. Since then, Lydia's friend, the sea captain, has helped me with it. As with the first letter, he says it's written in Celtic language. He's even heard it spoken ... but he says it sounds mighty strange compared to the way the Celts speak it ...maybe it's something about the weather there, or <u>the smoke in the mountains</u>.

Paul:
'Mighty strange' is hard to imagine, Timothy. The Celts talk funny enough as it is ...
[They both chuckle ...]
... But what does the letter say?

Timothy:
Well, it begins like the first one ...

> *'Grace, mercy and peace from God the Father and Christ Jesus our Lord.'*

Paul:
Ah, yes ... I remember. I like that!

Timothy:
And once again, it is written by 'Committee' ... actually, 'Celebration Committee'.

And it seems the church has a group of elders they call <u>the 'Church Council'</u>, and 'Committee' has been talking with <u>the Church Council</u>. They are excited about the celebration and your part in it ... <u>especially because of their name, St. Paul Evangelical Church.</u>"

Paul:
<u>*Well, my young friend, let's not revisit the name. We've been over that before. But*</u> *what else does the letter say?*

Timothy:
<u>*No, you don't need to remind me how much you dislike people naming churches after you. But it is odd, that Peter doesn't seem to mind churches being named after him.*</u>

[**Paul** shakes his head ... as **Timothy** continues]

<u>*Anyway,*</u> *I can see why they want you to come. As 'Committee' explains –*

> *'<u>Since the last winter solstice</u>, the church has been remembering its history. <u>In particular, we remember December 5 as a very important day because on that day many years ago, St. Paul Evangelical Church was officially organized as a congregation. That is why the first Sunday in December is the day we have picked to celebrate the history of our ministry.</u>*
>
> *'For the last few months, our education classes have been studying Luke's writings about Paul's missionary journeys, the challenge we share with you in proclaiming the good news of Jesus the*

> *Christ to a world longing to hear, and the excitement when the spark of the Holy Spirit bursts into flame in the heart of a believer.'*

Paul:
Ah, yes ... now I recall their first letter. And my encouragement to you, Timothy, to 'fan into flame the gift of God that is within you.' Do you remember our conversation?

Timothy:
Of course I do, because you reminded me that the gift within every believer is the Holy Spirit ... a Spirit not of timidity ... but of power, and of love, and of self-discipline. It took me a while to trust that truth, Paul, and to claim that flame. And it sounds like the believers <u>near the Mountains of Smoke</u> are beginning to trust it, too. Listen to the next part of the letter —

> *'But while we remember the saints who shaped <u>St. Paul Evangelical Church</u> and give thanks for its past and present ministries, the <u>Church Council</u> is challenging us to view the celebration as a springboard into God's intended future for the church.'*

In the rest of the letter, the 'Committee' shares details about the celebration plans ... and closes with this urgent plea:

> *'So dear Timothy, we implore you to prevail upon Paul on our behalf. His experience and insight ... to trust the Spirit and act on its guidance ... is just what we need.'*

[Paul is silent and contemplative. Timothy pauses to await Paul's response ... and then **Timothy** continues]: *Lydia's friend has a ship leaving next week to cross the Great Sea of the West. You would reach <u>the Mountains of Smoke</u> a few days before the celebration.*

[Paul sits silently for a moment, thinking. Timothy watches]
Paul [continues slowly]:
How long has it been, Timothy, since we were together in Jerusalem and you shared the first letter?

Timothy [thinks for a moment, then]:
It was in early spring, almost a year ago.

Paul [after pondering a bit]:
Though we've not met, the sisters and brothers at the church in <u>the land they call Teh-nah'-see</u> remind me of our many friends in the churches of Macedonia and Asia. How thankful we are to God for them.

But I'm also remembering the promise God made to Abraham long ago. 'I will bless you,' God said, 'and you will be a blessing.'

[Paul pauses to reflect … then continues]: *'I will bless you … and you will be a blessing.'*

[Another brief pause … then **Paul** continues]:
Since that first letter, I've visited with a number of people who have blessed me. You … Peter … Luke … your mother, Eunice.

'Blessed, to be a blessing,' God says.

That promise wasn't just for Abraham. God makes the same promise to every believer through all generations … to every saint. We are being blessed because of the saints who have gone before us.

The psalmist says, 'Taste and see that the Lord is good'. God's goodness flows into the world through the saints … saints of past generations, and saints who surround us today. This promise of God … blessed, to be a blessing … is for you and for me, Timothy. It is for the saints of <u>St. Paul Evangelical Church in the land of Teh-nah'-see</u>. And the promise is for the saints in God's intended future there, too.

'Blessed … to be a blessing'.

It is an important reminder for the saints in <u>the land of Teh-nah'-see</u> as they ponder God's intended future. That they have been blessed … and that they are the blessing for those they will never know … so that those who come after them will also be able to 'taste and see that the Lord is good.'

Timothy [pauses to ponder ... then]:
So, Paul, it sounds like your message to the saints gathered as the church in <u>Teh-nah'-see</u> is to 'taste and see' the goodness of God as they celebrate the blessings they have received."

Paul:
Yes, that is true ... and that is important. But read to me again, what the letter says ... the part about what the <u>Church Council</u> is asking ...

Timothy [pauses to scan the letter ... then]:
Ok ... here it is, I think ...

'But while we remember the saints who shaped <u>St. Paul Evangelical Church</u>, and give thanks for its past and present ministries, the <u>Church Council</u> is challenging us to view the celebration as a springboard into God's intended future for the church.'

Is that the part you mean?

Paul:
That's it! It sounds like this '<u>Church Council</u>' is challenging each believer to live into the intended future God has for each one of them ... and to know that as they do, ministries of the church will flourish in ways beyond their imagining. And as they are being blessed, so the generations that follow will be blessed.

Each person ... blessed, to be a blessing. The church ... blessed, to be a blessing.

Timothy:
I wonder how they will do that. I mean, I get the challenge by <u>the Church Council</u> to each believer. But I wonder ... how they will do it? [He stares into the distance, thinking ... then continues, slowly]

How does a believer go about living into the 'intended future' God has for him, or for her?

[Timothy is staring blankly toward the audience ... as Paul watches Timothy. Gradually, Timothy turns to Paul ... and repeats the question.]

How does a believer go about living into the 'intended future' God has for him, or for her?

[Paul remains silent, watching Timothy ... wearing an expression of encouragement and expectation. After a pause, the answer comes to Timothy ...]

'Fan into flame! Fan into flame ...!'

Paul [smiles broadly, looking at Timothy]:
And ...?

Timothy [proudly continuing]:
Fan into flame the gift of God that is within you ...

[Timothy pauses, waiting for Paul to speak. Paul remains silent, so Timothy continues]

... For you have been given a Spirit not of timidity ... but of power, and of love, and of self-discipline.

Paul:
You remember my letter well, Timothy. So what does it mean? How does a believer go about living into God's 'intended future'? What would you tell the saints in <u>the land they call Teh-nah'-see, near the Mountains of Smoke</u>?

Timothy [turns thoughtful]:
Hmmm ... well, I guess I would encourage them, just as you have encouraged me, to fan the into flame this gift, this Spirit. To get past the timidity of stepping out. Instead, to step boldly into their faith. To trust the Spirit ... to Claim the Flame ... to believe in its power.

I'm not sure though, Paul ... because for me, the hardest part is still getting past the timidity. Oh, yes ... I have seen the power of the Spirit. Sometimes I have even felt the power. But the timidity is a constant in my life ... it's a constant battle. And before you say it ... yes, I know this has to do with the 'self-discipline' piece. But it is a battle.

Paul:
It is a battle for every believer, Timothy ... for me, too. That is why it is important to encourage each other in the battle.

[Paul pauses ... then continues]:
But our conversation, and your words here, remind me of something Peter and John told me years ago. They were remembering when they were first getting to know Jesus and each other. They were all sitting on a hillside, and Jesus was teaching them about living the way God desires. He described what it would be like if everything was just the way God intends, and he began by saying, 'Blessed are the poor in spirit, for theirs is the kingdom of heaven.' There was a lot more to Jesus' teaching that day, and as they were recalling, John said something I'll never forget. John said that 'we are all children of God, and what we will be has not yet been made known.'

So ... the saints ... blessed, to be a blessing ... God's intended future ... the Spirit, God's gift within us ... what we will be, not yet made known.

[Paul pauses ...]

Timothy:
And ...?

Paul [chuckles, and continues]:
You have learned well, my young friend.

[Both chuckle... and Paul continues]

Blessed, to be a blessing.

Blessed, are the poor in spirit ... the impoverished of spirit ... the empty of spirit.

Remember hearing of the time when Jesus told the rich young man to give everything away and follow Him? By giving away all he had and becoming 'poor', Jesus was encouraging him to surrender everything ... to surrender himself completely.
To be 'poor in spirit' means to surrender our self-will completely, to become 'poor in spirit' ... so that in our emptiness, our poverty ... we are filled with God's will and not our own. When we surrender completely, we are filled.

So to step into God's intended future means to trust the nudge of the Spirit ... to fan into flame that nudge. To Claim the Flame. To step beyond timidity, and trust the power, the love, and the self-discipline of the Spirit.

'Blessed are the poor in spirit, for theirs is the kingdom of heaven.' Full citizens of the kingdom, as children of God ... what we will be, being made known.

Timothy:
So for the church in <u>the land of Ten-nah'-see</u> ... to step into God's intended future for <u>St. Paul Evangelical Church</u> ... it is as simple as each believer surrendering to the nudge of the Spirit?

Paul:
Yes, Timothy ... as simple as that. And that will be your message to them when you visit.

Timothy:
My message?!!? When I visit? No, Paul ... they have asked for you. I'm just the messenger. You are the Apostle, the evangelist. <u>Besides that, the church bears your name</u>. They want you.

Paul:
I am old, Timothy. Luke is right. I have one long trip left in me, and that will be to Rome. The believers <u>near the Mountains of Smoke</u> will understand.

No, it is your time. You are the next generation in the faith, and it is your time to step up ... just as it is time for the next generation in the faith, in <u>the land they call Teh-nah'-see</u>, to step up.

They have been blessed by the saints who have gone before. It is their time to build upon the foundation that has been laid for them, to bless the saints yet to come. They will understand.

Timothy:
Well ... I guess I feared this time would come some day. I have one concern, though ... and that is, to be back in time to accompany you to Rome. Luke says it is very important that we be with you ... and I have pledged to myself to do that.

Paul:
Go, my son. And tell the believers gathered as <u>St. Paul Evangelical Church</u> that I have been blessed by them these last months ... since their first letter arrived. Because of them, I have visited old friends and reclaimed the flame within me.

[They stand, and embrace. Paul continues ...]

Go in peace. Serve the Lord.

Timothy:
Thanks be to God.

[Timothy walks casually down the aisle as Paul watches him leave. Then, Paul departs.]

The Letter: *Greetings and Encouragement*

To prepare for the concluding sermon or address at the Celebration event by the keynote speaker, a handwritten letter from Timothy (along with the seven dialogue scripts) may be mailed to the speaker several weeks beforehand. The speaker may consider using parts or all of the letter in the keynote address.

Adaptation: *Modify all underscored dialogue to adapt to local context.*

Timothy, a follower of Christ Jesus, and Paul and Luke, our brothers also in Christ,

To <u>Julian</u>, our fellow worker in the Lord, and to our brothers and sisters across the Great Sea of the West in <u>the land they call Teh-nah'-see near the Mountains of Smoke</u>:

Grace to you and peace from God our Father and the Lord Jesus Christ.

We have thrilled in reading your letters from <u>St. Paul Evangelical Church</u>, and daily give thanks to God for the Spirit in your hearts. Through you, God is breathing new life into the community you serve. Praise and thanks be to God! We hold you in our prayers constantly.

Our dear friend, Paul, has been greatly moved by your letters – <u>though he bristled on learning that his name has been claimed for your church.</u> But knowing that you are Evangelical and proclaiming the Christ pleases him.

When last with him, he instructed me to come to you in his place. The years have taken their toll, and he must conserve his strength for the coming trip to Rome.

But I am concerned for Paul, and cannot leave him in these days and weeks of his preparation.

And so, dear <u>Julian</u>, Paul and I charge you in our stead to convey warm wishes and prayers to the saints in <u>the land of Teh-nah'-see</u> as they remember the saints who have gone before them.

And with encouragement and admonishment, to remind them to constantly *fan into flame* the gift of God that is within them. For it is through the power of the Spirit that they will be the blessing of the saints yet to come.

The Lord be with your Spirit. Grace be with you.

About the Author

"Grampa likes to go fishing with me, but we don't catch very many. And when we're camping and its real dark and we're in the tent, he tells scary stories!

And he likes to roast hot dogs and cook beans over the campfire, but he doesn't like pineapple. And he likes to hunt dragons with me, and watch Star Wars.

And, oh yeah – he likes to take long walks and watch me ride my bike!"

-Ethan, grandson of the author.

Larry Moeller enjoys life in Maryville, Tennessee nestled against the Smoky Mountains.

Eighteen years in the corporate world, followed by over twenty years as co-founder and owner of a small business which helps clients succeed has given him a deep appreciation for and love of people.

He is a simple and grateful man.

<u>Works by Larry Moeller</u>
Claim the Flame © 2015
The Query © 2015

Acknowledgements

With grateful appreciation for:

The worshiping community of St. Paul Evangelical Lutheran Church in Maryville, Tennessee, who enthusiastically returned month after month to endure the whims and artistic license of the author. Thank you.

Pastor Rick Ohsiek and his insights as the stories unfolded, and his gracious relinquishing of the pulpit through the seven-part series. Thank you.

The encouragement of the co-members of the 60th Anniversary Committee: Ann, Carolyn, Gene, Helen, Merl, and Sally. Thank you.

Jacqueline Conzemius' artistry, and Sue Tyler's collaboration, in creating the flame emblem. Thank you.

The gifted thespians who brought the characters to life in their 2014 debut: Art and Tom (Paul); Ethan and John (Timothy); Pastor Rick (Peter); Liz (Lydia); Bryan (Luke); James (Ethiopian eunuch); Darla (Eunice). Thank you.

Brother Julian, whose Celebration message and greeting from Timothy proclaimed the blessing and challenge of living into God's intended future. Thank you, Brother Julian (aka, The Rev. H. Julian Gordy, bishop of the Southeastern Synod, Evangelical Lutheran Church in America).

The courage of the 1st century church and the boldness of Paul … who exhorts you and me to fan into flame the gift of God that is within you … for you have been given a Spirit not of timidity, but of power, and of love, and of self-discipline.

The love of God in Christ Jesus, our Lord.

www.ingramcontent.com/pod-product-compliance
Lightning Source LLC
Chambersburg PA
CBHW052202110526
44591CB00012B/2047